"WHAT HAVE I DONE"

A HUNTER'S REMEMBRANCE OF TAKING THE LIFE OF HIS FIRST DEER

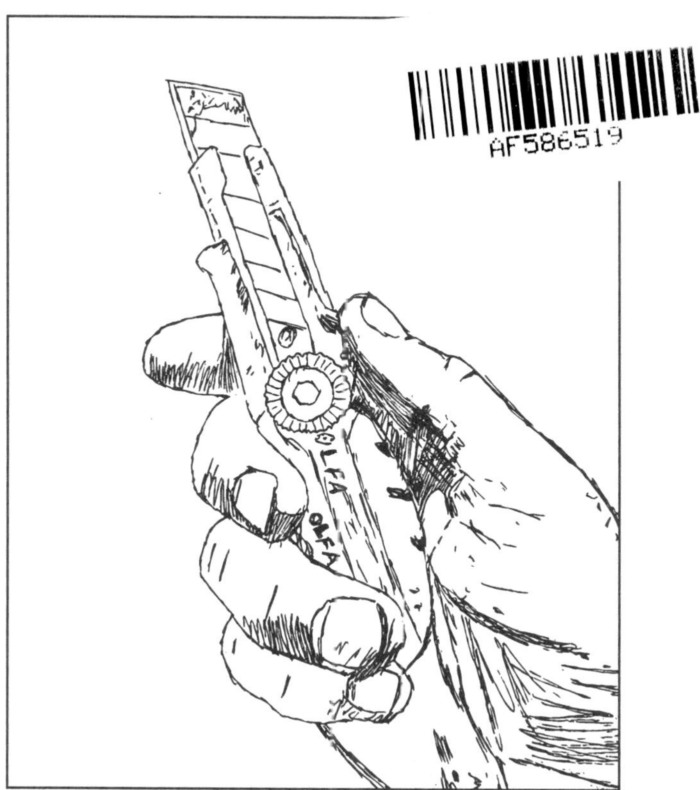

ISAAC W. HAINES

1st Printing, 2024 First Edition
Written By Isaac Haines
Edited by Aubry Haines

Flagstaff County, AB CANADA

ISBN
Soft Cover: 978-1-0690479-1-5
Hard Cover: 978-1-0690479-0-8

Graphic Content Warning

The story you are about to read is a true account of a hunter's experience killing his first deer. The events described are raw and unfiltered, containing graphic and gruesome scenes that may be distressing to some readers. Reader discretion is advised.

"What Have I Done"

A Hunter's Remembrance
of Harvesting His First Deer

Original artwork
by the author

Prologue

This is a true story about how I took the life of my first deer. I'll tell you exactly what happened. I won't flex on nothing. I took the life of an innocent young buck. I sliced open his throat with a yellow utility knife. I felt the vitality leave his body. I heard the blood build up in his lungs as he gurgled for breath.

This is not a beautiful story. It was an unnecessary killing: there's a Wendy's down the road from my house, I wasn't starving, I didn't need to kill this animal.

But I did..

and I'd do it again.

And I'll tell you why.

November 23rd, 2022.

5:40 a.m.

I park the car. Ice is on the ground; freezing rain fell overnight. The temperature is supposed to drop today. But for now, in the shrouded darkness, it's warm. I grab my gun, my bag, and that's it. I wish I had more "stuff," but I'm new to this. I don't really know what the hell I'm doing. I've never done this before. I've never killed anything bigger than a fish. I've never felt warm blood run down my hands.

My father didn't hunt, nor did my grandfather. I'm doing this on my own, and I can't even really explain why -much like, I couldn't explain why I started fishing all those years ago.

I was always by the creek as a child -I was just drawn to it. My brothers always gathered around the Xbox or Nintendo, and I'll admit, Halo was lit. But other than that, I was never much for "games" or "inside" activities.

My parents took us camping; they showed me the mountains and the foothills. My feet melded to the hills from a young age. As I grew older, I wanted more of it. I bought my first spinning rod when I was 19. The next year, that rod turned into a fly rod. For over a decade, I caught fish all around Alberta; I was obsessed with it. But I soon noticed myself looking for more again.

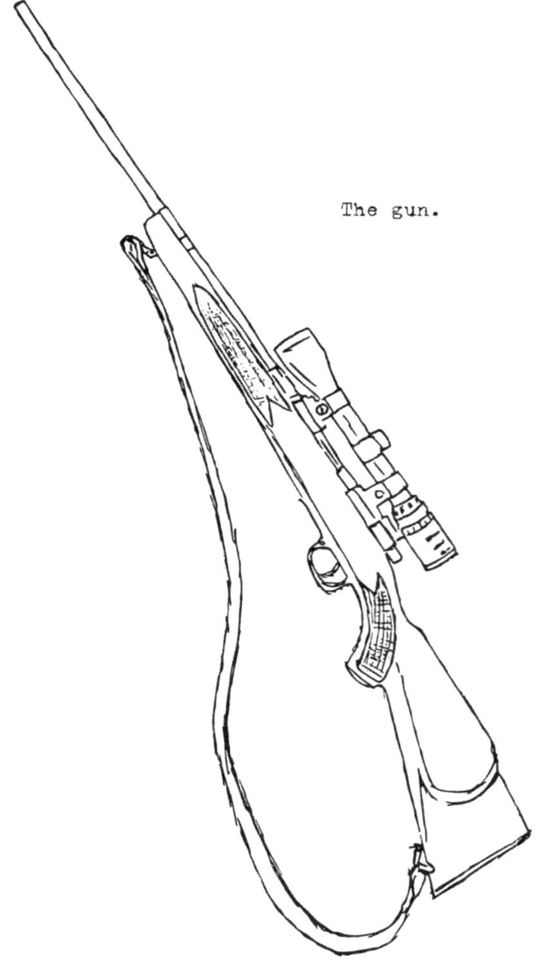

The gun.

What a terrible thing. What a brutal device. And yet, in the right hands, what an efficient tool. I could say more about guns, but I won't.

I start walking. The darkness surrounds me. It feels, private. It feels... comforting. I can still see the stars, my eyes slowly adjusting to the dimness. After a while, I can see everything

"What Have I Done"

I've been here scouting a few times. I saw some deer using what looked like a channel, going from one field to the next. My plan was to set up at one end and just wait. I didn't think my plan would be successful, so I brought a thermos full of coffee to help pass the time. When I got to where I was going, I found a good log to sit on. I check my gun -it's unloaded. I have three bullets in my chest pocket. I unzip it, pull one out, and I just stare at it.

It's a .30-06 cartridge. I feel different towards it. Partially for its size. Partially because I'm not used to it. But mostly, for the thought of what it can do- the damage it can bestow and the sheer destruction it can leave in its wake, especially if the discharge is unintentional. God forbid my finger ever slips.

Isaac W. Haines

I didn't think I would see a deer, let alone shoot a deer, or even kill a deer for that matter. But as I raised my eyes from the brass cartridge and looked across the field, four hundred yards away, I saw a dark shadow moving across the cut wheat. I blinked and leaned forward, trying to focus.

Yes, dawn was coming, but it was not here yet, and the light was still low.

It took a second, but my mind finally processed what I saw: it was, in fact, a deer.

My heart skipped a beat. It was moving at a steady pace, headed for the forest. It was about to jump a fence and be gone. So I stood up, placed my hands around my mouth, and made what was probably the worst deer call you can imagine. But, to my surprise, the deer stopped in its tracks and looked in my direction.

I thought I saw it walk towards me. But then, like in a blink, it vanished. It was too far away to see, but I couldn't see it no more. I stayed silent, watching and hoping it would return. My heart was pounding. My gun was in my hands. I loaded three bullets...

just in case.

I look at my phone.

Ten minutes to legal light.

All of a sudden the deer shows itself again. It's closer... much closer. Maybe half the distance it was. I can't believe it. I let out another deer call using my mouth -I probably sound like a wounded cow. But I don't care. I later learned it was prime rut, and this young buck was curious.

As fast as it showed itself, it disappears again, weaving its way in and out of the brush and trees. I look at my phone. **Three minutes** 'til legal light.

I'm waiting...

Less than one hundred yards away, the buck steps out again. My heart rate picks up. My whole body tenses. I look at my phone.
One minute 'til legal light. I have him in my scope-his lungs are in my crosshairs and my hand is placed against the tree as a rest. He's walking towards me. I'm worried he will get too close. I'm worried he'll smell me. I'm worried he'll sense me.

"What Have I Done"

I look at my phone.

8:13 a.m.

I pull the trigger.

He falls down.

I run up to him.

"What Have I Done"

I kneel down in front of him, my heart pounding. A wave of guilt and horror washes over me. Although I aimed for his lungs, in my shakiness, I was too high and caught him in the spine. He's down, but trying to get up. His eyes are wide, full of life, staring right into mine. I can see his 'will to live', I can feel his agony, his fear, his sorrow-maybe I'm projecting. But I started something, and now I had to finish it.

Acting completely primal; I reach for my shoulder pocket where I kept a yellow OFLA utility knife. I run at him, jump on his back, grab his antlers, and with my right hand, slice open his jugular. I hear a rush of air come out, his body jolt, and his head jerk back. This was not safe. In hindsight, I should've just put a bullet through his heart, but at the time, I didn't think about that. I was acting only out of instinct.

I wish I could tell you;

when you slice open a deer's throat, it dies immediately. Looking back, it was probably just a minute. But that minute felt like a lifetime. All I wanted was for it to be over-for the suffering to be done. But while it was gurgling, gasping for breath, heart beating,

it was alive

His breath slows,
Its head now resting in the snow.

I keep saying to myself
"I'm sorry, I'm sorry, I'm sorry."

I didn't know it would be like this. I didnt think it would be this brutal.

My right hand covered in blood, my body tired from all the torture I'm afflicting.

All I want is for the gurgling to stop. But still, it continues. To this day, this terrible sound is still with me.

But eventually, everything goes quiet. Its chest stops rising. Its life, its spirit, all at once, leave its body.

I stand up, shaky and shocked. I notice his eyes. They'er completely different. They're, 'lifeless': black with a cloudy white glaze over them. There's nothing there anymore.

I've just taken the life of something that wanted to live and did not deserve to die. I feel terrible. I feel like I have done something wrong. I feel like I have committed murder...

I look at my hand, bloody, still clenching the yellow utility knife.

and I think to myslef; "what have I done"

"What Have I Done"

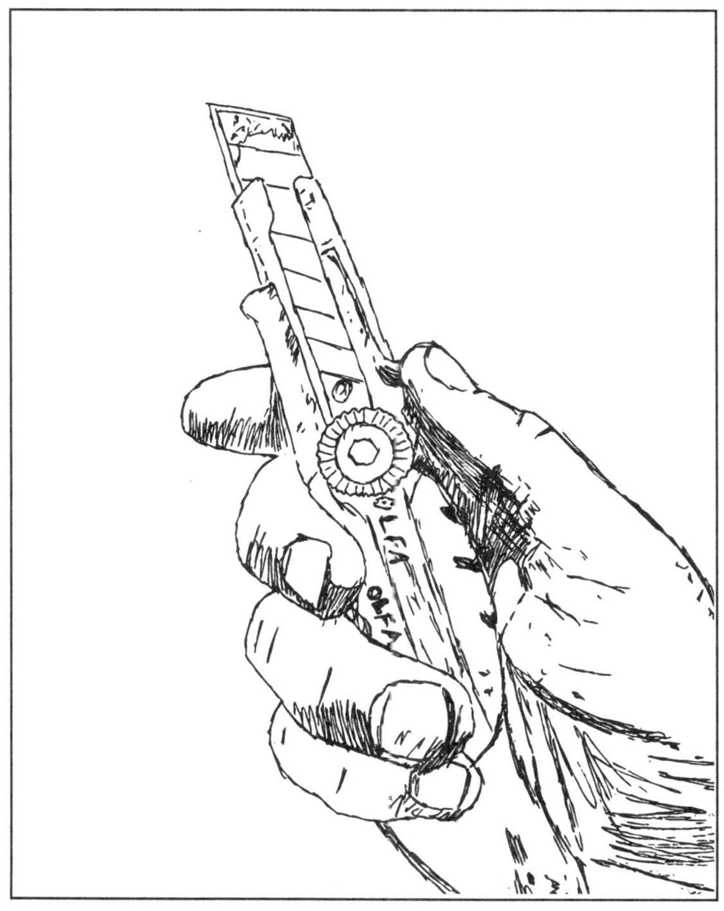

what have I done

"What Have I Done"

what have I done

If you grow up with this,
maybe it's different.

If you're around hunters,
maybe it's different.

If you've done this a hundred times,
maybe it's different.

But if this world is
completely new to you,

it's strange.

However,

if this is the true cost of protein,
then let me pay for it, year over year
year over year.

If life must be removed in order for our bodies to be sustained, then let me take that life myself.

If there must be death,
in order for there to be life,
then let me see it.
Let the blood fall on my hands
and no one else's.

Let me be the hunter
that pays the price.

"What Have I Done"

Is a true story
Written by Isaac Haines
August 20, 2024

"What Have I Done"

Acknowledgments and Homage

Clare Butterfly

There are two people in particular I need to credit for the success of my first harvest.

Clair Butterfly, for taking me out hunting twice, allowing me to purchase his old .30-06, and generously gifting me plenty of ammo. He showed me many things while in the field with him, as well as showing me how to sight in the rifle. He also taught me how to make a deer call with my hands and mouth, which I used to call in the deer. Without your support, Clare, I wouldn't have harvested my deer that day.

Jazz O'Driscoll

I also want to thank my good friend, Jazz O'Driscoll.
Jazz has always been an incredible source of knowledge and a sounding board for any questions. Throughout my entire fishing, and now hunting, journey, he has graciously and openly shared his expertise with me. Additionally, he provided the location of the grazing lease where I harvested this deer. If it weren't for Jazz, I wouldn't have harvested that deer that day.

Thank you both.

Aubry Haines

Big thank you to my brother, Aubry
You took the time to edit and proof this book. I know this is something you do professionally, every day. And so for you to take the time and energy to read and offer some amazing edits meant the world to me.

If it were not for you, I am quite positive this book would be lacking in some much-needed grammar and punctuation.

You also made some lovely notes which I took to heart.

Thank you

You, the reader

Books are written to be read.
A book is nothing if no one reads it.

So from the bottom of my heart, I would like to thank you -the reader.

Whoever you are, wherever you are.
Thank you.

I hope you will not be a ghost to me. If you enjoyed this book. Or if something touched you in any way, I ask that you would do me a favour and send me an email.

I of course will read it, and I promise I will respond to each one

mr.isaachaines@gmail.com

Kindly,

- Isaac Haines

"What Have I Done"

Isaac W. Haines

2024

www.ingramcontent.com/pod-product-compliance
Lightning Source LLC
LaVergne TN
LVHW052106160826
845678LV00015B/3387

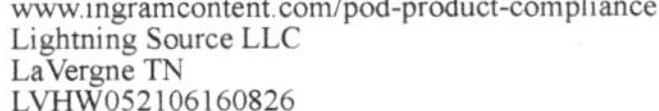

* 9 7 8 1 0 6 9 0 4 7 9 1 5 *